双双中文教材 (16)
Chinese Language and Culture Course

中国诗歌欣赏 Appreciation of Chinese Poetry

王双双 编著

北京大学出版社
PEKING UNIVERSITY PRESS

图书在版编目（CIP）数据

中国诗歌欣赏/王双双 编著.—北京：北京大学出版社，2007.3
（双双中文教材16）
ISBN 978-7-301-08707-7

Ⅰ.中… Ⅱ.王… Ⅲ.汉语-对外汉语教学-教材 Ⅳ.H195.4

中国版本图书馆CIP数据核字（2005）第075453号

书　　　　名：	中国诗歌欣赏
著作责任者：	王双双　编著
英文翻译：	王约西
责任编辑：	孙　娴
标准书号：	ISBN 978-7-301-08707-7/H·1443
出版发行：	北京大学出版社
地　　　　址：	北京市海淀区成府路205号　100871
网　　　　址：	http://www.pup.cn
电　　　　话：	邮购部 62752015　发行部 62750672　编辑部 62752028　出版部 62754962
电子信箱：	zpup@pup.pku.edu.cn
印　　刷　　者：	北京大学印刷厂
经　　销　　者：	新华书店
	889毫米×1194毫米　16开本　9.25印张　165千字
	2007年3月第1版　2018年8月第5次印刷
定　　　　价：	78.00元（含课本、练习册和CD-ROM盘一张）

未经许可，不得以任何方式复制或抄袭本书之部分或全部内容。
版权所有，侵权必究
举报电话：（010）62752024
电子信箱：fd@pup.pku.edu.cn

前言

《双双中文教材》是一套专门为海外青少年编写的中文课本，是我在美国八年的中文教学实践基础上编写成的。在介绍这套教材之前，请读一首小诗：

> 一双神奇的手，
> 推开一扇窗。
> 一条神奇的路，
> 通向灿烂的中华文化。
>
> 鲍凯文 鲍维江
> 1998年

鲍维江和鲍凯文姐弟俩是美国生美国长的孩子，也是我的学生。1998年冬，他们送给我的新年贺卡上的小诗，深深地打动了我的心。我把这首诗看成我文化教学的"回声"。我要传达给海外每位中文老师：我教给他们（学生）中国文化，他们思考了、接受了、回应了。这条路走通了！

语言是交际的工具，更是一种文化和一种生活方式，所以学习中文也就离不开中华文化的学习。汉字是一种古老的象形文字，她从远古走来，带有大量的文化信息，但学起来并不容易。使学生增强兴趣、减小难度，走出苦学汉字的怪圈，走进领悟中华文化的花园，是我编写这套教材的初衷。

学生不论大小，天生都有求知的欲望，都有欣赏文化美的追求。中华文化本身是魅力十足的。把这宏大而玄妙的文化，深入浅出地，有声有色地介绍出来，让这迷人的文化如涓涓细流，一点一滴地渗入学生们的心田，使学生们逐步体味中国文化，是我编写这套教材的目的。

为此我将汉字的学习放入文化介绍的流程之中同步进行，让同学们在学中国地理的同时，学习汉字；在学中国历史的同时，学习汉字；在学中国哲学的同时，学习汉字；在学中国科普文选的同时，学习汉字……

这样的一种中文学习，知识性强，趣味性强；老师易教，学生易学。当学生们合上书本时，他们的眼前是中国的大好河山，是中国五千年的历史和妙不可言的哲学思维，是奔腾的现代中国……

总之，他们了解了中华文化，就会探索这片土地，热爱这片土地，就会与中国结下情缘。

最后我要衷心地感谢所有热情支持和帮助我编写教材的老师、家长、学生、朋友和家人，特别是老同学唐玲教授、何茜老师、我姐姐王欣欣编审及我女儿Uta Guo年复一年的鼎力相助。可以说这套教材是大家努力的结果。

王双双
2005年5月8日

说明

《双双中文教材》是一套专门为海外学生编写的中文教材。它是由美国加州王双双老师和中国专家学者共同努力，在海外多年的实践中编写出来的。全书共20册，识字量2500个，包括了从识字、拼音、句型、短文的学习，到初步的较系统的中国文化的学习。教材大体介绍了中国地理、历史、哲学等方面的丰富内容，突出了中国文化的魅力。课本知识面广，趣味性强，深入浅出，易教易学。

这套教材体系完整、构架灵活、使用面广。学生可以从零起点开始，一直学完全部课程20册；也可以将后11册（10～20册）的九个文化专题和第五册（汉语拼音）单独使用，这样便于高中和大学开设中国哲学、地理、历史等专门课程以及假期班、短期中国文化班、拼音速成班使用，符合了美国AP中文课程的目标和基本要求。

本书是《双双中文教材》的第十六册，适用于已学习掌握约1200个汉字的学生使用。本书选取了大量古代著名诗词和部分当代诗歌，所选皆为名作，各具风格。这些诗词有描述民间生活的艰辛困苦，有抒发英雄的悲壮豪情，有对恋人的深情表白，也有对大好江山的赞叹。集中介绍诗词的目的是让学生欣赏中国诗词特有的韵律美，体会中国诗词，特别是中国古典诗词表达情感时的丰富表现力，同时，学生们也能形象地了解中国古代社会生活的点滴。

编者

课程设置

一年级	中文课本（第一册）	中文课本（第二册）	中文课本（第三册）
二年级	中文课本（第四册）	中文课本（第五册）	中文课本（第六册）
三年级	中文课本（第七册）	中文课本（第八册）	中文课本（第九册）
四年级	中国成语故事	中国地理常识	
五年级	中国古代故事	中国神话传说	
六年级	中国古代科学技术	中国文学欣赏	
七年级	中国诗歌欣赏	中文科普阅读	
八年级	中国古代哲学	中国历史（上）	
九年级	中国历史（下）	小说阅读，中文SAT II	
十年级	中文SAT II（强化班）	小说阅读，中文SAT II考试	

目录

第一课　诗经与楚辞 …………………………… 1

第二课　乐府 …………………………… 10

第三课　唐诗（一）…………………………… 24

第四课　唐诗（二）…………………………… 33

第五课　唐诗（三）…………………………… 40

第六课　宋词（一）…………………………… 46

第七课　宋词（二）…………………………… 53

第八课　宋词（三）…………………………… 62

第九课　古诗词二首 …………………………… 68

第十课　现代诗二首 …………………………… 75

生字表 …………………………… 85

生词表 …………………………… 89

第一课

诗经与楚辞

诗 经

《诗经》是中国第一部诗歌总集,相传由孔子和他的学生所编,最后编定成书大约在公元前6世纪。《诗经》原名《诗》,或称《诗三百》,共收集诗歌305篇,包括从西周初至春秋中叶五百多年间流传的社会各个阶层人士的作品。作品内容十分广泛,反映了当时社会生活的方方面面。

《诗经》是中国古代诗歌的起点,对中国后世的诗歌影响深远。

采 葛

彼采葛兮,一日不见,如三月兮!
彼采萧(xī)兮,一日不见,如三秋兮!
彼采艾兮,一日不见,如三岁兮!

【注释】

葛:植物名,花紫红色,根可作药用。
彼:那、那个;对方、他(她)。

兮：助词，跟现代文的"啊"相似。

萧：植物名，即青蒿(hāo)，有香气。

艾：植物名，叶子有香气，可用作药材。

【诗文讲解】

这是《诗经》中一首爱情诗歌。文中描写了情人分离的思念和痛苦：

那个姑娘采葛去了，我一天没有见到她，就像隔了三个月呀！

那个姑娘采萧去了，我一天没有见到她，就像隔了三个季度那样长啊！

那个姑娘采艾去了，我一天没有见到她，就像隔了三年那样长又长呀！

这首诗短短几句，就把想念情人越来越强烈的心情生动地表现出来了。至今人们仍然用"一日不见，如隔三秋"来形容强烈的思念之情。

屈原与楚辞

屈原（约前340—前278）是战国时期楚国人，中国历史上第一位伟大的诗人。他创造了一种新的诗歌形式——楚辞。楚辞与《诗经》共同构成了中国诗歌的源头。

楚辞是在南方浪漫民风的影响下，在民歌的基础上发展起来的，诗句由自由的长短句构成。句中、句尾常用"兮"字表示语气。这样的诗体新鲜、生动，富有表现力。

屈原一生写出了许多优秀的诗歌，其中最著名的是《离骚》。

《离骚》是中国古代最长的一首抒情诗。在《离骚》中，作者写出了自己不幸的一生和被放逐后的悲愤心情，以及对楚国人民的热爱之情。如：

长太息以掩涕兮,(我长叹一声禁不住流下眼泪啊,)

哀民生之多艰!(可怜人民的生活这样多灾多难!)

……

路漫漫其修远兮,(我要走的路是多么漫长啊,)

吾将上下而求索。(我将上天入地去追求我的理想。)

《离骚》不但感情奔放,想象浪漫神奇,而且语句美丽动人。楚辞的产生与屈原一生的遭遇和他高洁的品格是分不开的。

屈原出生在楚国一个贵族家庭。那时楚国在长江、汉水流域,是一个有五千里山河的大国。屈原早年受楚怀王信任和重用,做过高官。他主张联合其他国家共同抵抗强大的秦国。没想到楚怀王不但没有采用他的主张,反而把他放逐了。屈原在被放逐的生活中时刻关心着楚国的命运。看到他热爱的楚国一天天衰落,一次次被秦军打败,他悲痛万分,写出了《离骚》、《九歌》、《天问》等诗歌来表达内心的痛苦。最后,屈原眼见着秦军占领了楚国的都城,楚国灭亡了。他悲痛到极点,在农历五月初五投汨(mì)罗江自杀。

相传,老百姓们听说他投江以后,马上划船去救他,可是没有打捞到屈原。为了不让他的尸体被鱼吃掉,人们往江里撒米喂鱼。从此以后,人们为了纪念屈原,每年农历五月五日都要赛龙船、吃粽子,过端午节。

生 词

shōu jí 收集	collect	bēi fèn 悲愤	grief and indignation
piān 篇	chapter	yǎn 掩	cover
guǎng fàn 广泛	wide-ranging	tì 涕	tears
fǎn yìng 反映	reflect	jīn bu zhù 禁不住	can not restrain; can't help (doing sth)
yǐng xiǎng 影响	affect; influence	qiú suǒ 求索	seek
bǐ 彼	that; she; he	zhuī qiú 追求	chase
ài 艾	mugwort	lǐ xiǎng 理想	ideal
xíng shì 形式	form	zāo yù 遭遇	suffering
làng màn 浪漫	romantic	guì zú 贵族	nobles; aristocrat
jī chǔ 基础	basis; foundation	mìng yùn 命运	fate; destiny
lí sāo 离骚	*The Sorrow of Departure (Lisao)*	shuāi luò 衰落	decline
shū qíng 抒情	express one's emotion	jì niàn 纪念	commemorate
fàng zhú 放逐	banish; exile	zòng zi 粽子	*a food made of glutinous rice wrapped in bamboo leaves*

听写

广泛　形式　基础　反映　遭遇　放逐　悲愤　掩

求索　浪漫　纪念　＊粽子　抒情

注：＊以后的字词为选做题，后同。

比一比

构 { 构成 / 结构　　遇 { 遭遇 / 遇到　　仍 { 仍然 / 仍旧

基 { 基础 / 基本　　漫 { 浪漫 / 漫长　　形 { 形式 / 形状

字词运用

构成　结构

《楚辞》与《诗经》共同构成了中国诗歌的源头。

赵州桥是拱形结构的。

浪漫　漫长

《牛郎织女》是一个浪漫的民间故事。

中国北方的冬季十分漫长。

回答问题

1. 中国历史上第一部诗歌总集叫什么？
2. 《诗经》编定成书大约是在什么时候？
3. 中国诗歌的源头是哪两部作品？
4. 《诗经》共有诗歌多少篇？
5. 中国历史上第一位伟大的诗人是谁？
6. 屈原是战国时期哪国人？
7. 请说一说中国的端午节是怎么来的。

词语解释

中叶——一个历史时期的中段。

热爱——强烈地爱，非常爱。

构成——形成；造成；结构。

民歌——民间口头流传的歌曲。

纪念——对人或事表示怀念。

作品——文学艺术方面加工好的成品，如：出版的书籍、上演的影片。

Lesson One

Shijing and Chuci

Shijing

Shijing (The Book of Odes) is the earliest collection of Chinese poems. It's said to be compiled by Confucias and his studeats.Completed in the form of a book in approximately the sixth century B.C., it was originally called *Shi* (Poems) or *Shisanbai* (Three Hundred Poems). Covering more than five hundred years from the early Zhou Dynasty to the middle of the Spring and Autumn Period, *Shijing* includes 305 popular poems and verses written by people of all social levels. With its wide-ranging contents, *Shijing* reflects all perspectives of the social life of that time.

Shijing is the starting point of Chinese ancient poems and verses and has exerted a deep and powerful influence on the Chinese poetry of later ages.

Collecting Kudsu

My lass is away collecting kudsu,
I haven't seen her for one day only,
But it seems as long as three months truly!

My lass is away collecting mugwort,
I haven't seen her for one day only,
But it seems as long as three seasons truly!

My lass is away collecting wormwood,
I haven't seen her for one day only,
But it seems as long as three years truly!

Qu Yuan and Chuci

Qu Yuan (app. 340 – 278 B.C.) is the first great poet in the history of China. A poet of the Chu State, he created a new form of poem – chuci (a type of classical Chinese literature and a form of classical poetry typical for its local Character of the Chu State). Chuci and *Shijing* co-constitute the origin of Chinese poetry and verse.

Affected by the romantic folk customs of south China, chuci developed on the base of folk songs which consist mostly of long and short lines. In or at the end of the lines there often appears the character 兮 that makes a tone. This style of poems is fresh, vivid and expressive.

In his life, Qu Yuan wrote many excellent poems and verses. *Lisao* (the Sorrow of Departure) is one of the most well known.

In *Lisao*, the longest lyric poem in ancient China, the poet depicts his unfortunate life, his grief and indignation, and his ardent love for the Chu people. For example:

> With a deep and long sigh of woe
> I can't stop my tears from falling;
> It's for people's misery and sorrow
> That I often go bitterly weeping.
>
> ......
>
> The road ahead for me is so long,
> Step by step I walk dragging along.
> To seek for ideal I'd adventure
> May it be happiness or torture.

Lisao is not only overflowing with enthusiasm and full of romantic and profound feelings, but with lovely and touching lines.

The birth of chuci is closely connected with Qu Yuan's misfortune in his life and his lofty character.

Qu Yuan was born in a noble family in the Chu State which was then a large country of five thousand leagues located along the Yangtze River and the Han River. Trusted by the King of Chu (named King Huai), he was once a very high official. Nevertheless, his suggestion that the Chu State unite other countries to oppose the Qin State was unexpectedly rejected by King Huai. What is more, he was banished. During his banishment, he never stopped worrying about the fate of Chu. When he saw his beloved country deteriorating day after day and the Chu army was defeated by the Qin's, he was painfully sad and produced *Lisao*, *Jiuge* (The Nine Songs) and *Tianwen* (Heavenly Questions) etc. by which he conveyed his deep sorrow and bitterness. Finally, the capital of Chu was besieged and occupied by the Qin army. Chu perished. The fall of his motherland brought him to his extreme grief and on the fifth day of the fifth lunar month, he killed himself in the Miluo River.

On hearing his death, people rushed to his rescue on boats but in vain. To protect his body from being eaten by fish, they fed the fish by throwing rice into the river. Ever since then, on that day, it has become a traditional festival – *Duanwujie* (the Dragon Boat Festival) to memorize Qu Yuan by eating zongzi and having dragon-boat races.

第二课

乐 府

乐府开始于汉代,是国家专管音乐的一个机构,负责从民间收集诗歌。收集到的诗歌叫"乐府民歌"。这些诗歌语言朴素、生动,内容十分广泛。其中最有名的是东汉末年的《孔雀东南飞》和南北朝时期的《木兰辞》等。后来,诗人们把"乐府"作为一种诗体,创作了很多乐府诗。

孔雀东南飞

《孔雀东南飞》是汉乐府民歌中最优秀的叙事长诗,作者不详。全诗340多句,说的是一对善良的青年焦仲卿(zhòngqīng)与刘兰芝之间纯真的爱情悲剧故事。千百年来,这首诗歌一直在民间流传,深

深地打动着人们的心。

诗歌开头为：

孔雀东南飞

五里一徘徊

一只孤独的孔雀在天空飞来飞去，寻找他失去的伴侣，久久不肯离去。人世间也有同样的故事。刘兰芝是一个美丽、勤劳、知书达礼的姑娘，诗中说她：

十三能织素

十四学裁衣

十五弹箜篌（kōng hóu）

十六诵诗书

十七岁的刘兰芝美若天仙，嫁给了小府吏焦仲卿，夫妻俩相亲相爱。可是焦仲卿为了工作经常外出，两人相见的日子不多。兰芝在家中天不亮就织布，三天织五匹布，婆婆还是不满意，常常为难她。诗中写道：

十七为君妇

心中常苦悲

君既为府吏

守节情不移

贱妾（jiàn qiè）留空房

相见常日稀

鸡鸣入机织

夜夜不得息

三日断五匹

大人故嫌迟

她实在受不了婆婆的逼迫，于是提出："既然婆婆看不上我，就请把我送回娘家吧。"焦仲卿跪在地上向母亲求情：兰芝没有过错，为什么要让她走？要是母亲不肯留她，非让她走，我一生不会再娶别人为妻了。不想母亲听了以后大怒，喝道："你竟敢不听我的！你怎么能替刘兰芝说话？"

焦仲卿没有办法，只好含泪送兰芝回家。分手时焦仲卿立下誓言，表示虽然兰芝暂时回了家，但是他以后一定会再来接兰芝。兰芝也向天发誓，一定等着焦仲卿。

不料兰芝回到娘家后没有多久，县令①听说兰芝美丽、善良，就来为儿子求婚。母亲问兰芝答应不答应，她含泪答道：

兰芝初还时

府吏见叮咛

结誓不别离

---

① 县令——县官。

母亲知道兰芝还等着焦仲卿，就让求婚的人走了。可是过了不久，太守①又来为儿子求婚。兰芝还是不动心。这次她哥哥不耐烦了，认为嫁给太守的儿子有钱、有地位，多么荣耀，为什么要等焦仲卿！在哥哥的逼迫下，兰芝只好答应了太守家的求婚。

焦仲卿听说后，心急如火，骑马来见兰芝。两人相见，泪如雨下，感到天地之大，却没有他们的立足之处。于是约定，既然今生不能做夫妻，就不如一死，黄泉②下相见！

分手后，太守家迎亲的队伍来了，热热闹闹的。兰芝在新婚之夜，痛不欲生，投水自尽。焦仲卿知道后，也上吊自杀了。诗中写道：

我命绝今日

魂去尸长留

揽（lǎn）裙脱丝履（lǚ）

举身赴清池

府吏闻此事

心知长别离

徘徊庭树下

自挂东南枝

---

① 太守：汉朝管理一个郡（jùn）的最高地方官。

② 黄泉：地下的泉水，指人死后埋葬的地方。

两家求合葬

合葬华山傍

东西植松柏

左右种梧桐(wú tóng)

枝枝相覆盖

叶叶相交通

中有双飞鸟

自名为鸳鸯(yuān yāng)

仰头相向鸣

夜夜达五更(gēng)

刘兰芝和焦仲卿死后，焦、刘两家把他们埋葬在一起，墓边种上了松柏和梧桐。这些树长成了一片浓阴覆盖的树林，而焦仲卿和刘兰芝死后化作林中双飞的鸳鸯，相亲相爱永不分开。

【注释】

箜篌：一种古代乐器。

君：对人的尊称。

贱妾：古代妻子对自己的称呼。

绝：（呼吸）停止，死亡。

揽：用手提或抱。

履：鞋。

鸳鸯：一种鸟，雌雄成对生活在水边。文学上常用来比喻夫妻。

五更：中国古代把一夜分为五更，到五更就到了清晨。

游子吟

［唐］孟郊

慈母手中线，游子身上衣。

临行密密缝，意恐迟迟归。

谁言寸草心，报得三春晖。

【注释】

临行：临走前。

意：心愿；心意。

迟：慢；晚。

晖：阳光。

【诗文讲解】

这是一首乐府诗。诗中描写慈爱的妈妈手里拿着针线，为要远行的儿子缝衣服。细针密线地缝呀，缝呀，生怕儿子一去几年，迟迟不归。难道说小草的心真的能报答春天的太阳带给它的光和热吗？儿女们怎能报答母亲的深情厚爱！

这首诗亲切而真诚地歌颂(qiè sòng)了伟大的母爱，唤起天下儿女们对母亲的感恩(ēn)之情。千百年来，它深深地感动着每一位读者。

作者简介

孟郊（751—814），唐代诗人。这首诗是他当了官后，回家去接母亲时所作。

生词

xù shì	叙事	narrate	bī pò	逼迫	force; compel
jiāo	焦	Jiao (*surname*)	dīng níng	叮咛	urge repeatly
liú lán zhī	刘兰芝	Liu Lanzhi (*name*)	shàng diào	上吊	hang oneself
chún zhēn	纯真	pure; sincere	hún	魂	soul
bēi jù	悲剧	tragedy	sōng bǎi	松柏	pine and cypress
pái huái	徘徊	linger about; roam	fù gài	覆盖	cover; overlap
bàn lǚ	伴侣	companion; partner	mái zàng	埋葬	bury
qín láo	勤劳	industrious; diligent	yín	吟	chant; sing
lǎng sòng	（朗）诵	read aloud; recite	mèng jiāo	孟郊	Meng Jiao (*name*)
jià	嫁	(*of a woman*) marry	cí mǔ	慈母	loving mother
fǔ lì	府吏	official; clerk	féng	缝	sew; stitch
wéi nán	为难	feel embarrassed	huī	晖	sunshine; sunlight
xián	嫌	dislike			

听写

叙　纯真　嫁　逼迫　朗诵　叮咛　勤劳　嫌　慈母

郊　松柏　芝　*徘徊　伴侣

中国诗歌欣赏

默 写

《游子吟》

比一比

诵（朗诵） 朗（朗诵） 覆（覆盖）
通（通过） 郎（女郎） 复（重复）

嫌（嫌弃） 吏（官吏） 徘（徘徊）
歉（道歉） 史（历史） 排（排队）

柏（柏树） 叮咛 缝衣服
泊（湖泊） 叮 叮咬 缝 石头缝

字词运用

朗诵

班里要开诗歌朗诵会。

老师让我们大声朗诵这篇课文。

爷爷朗诵诗歌特别有感情。

嫌

大家都嫌他做事太马虎。

哥哥、姐姐都嫌妹妹太娇气。

他总嫌自己长得矮小。

覆盖

白雪覆盖着大地。

几万年前黄土高原曾被树木和绿草覆盖着。

喜马拉雅(yǎ)山脉终年白雪覆盖。

为难

刘兰芝很勤劳，每天干很多活，可婆婆还是经常为难她。

你明明知道小妹妹怕狗，还带狗来，这不是为难她吗？

不耐烦

学习的时候一定要有耐心，绝对不能不耐烦。

多音字

切(qiè)　　　　切(qiē)

亲切(qiè)　　　刀切(qiē)

回答问题

1. 乐府开始于哪个朝代?

2. 请说出两首最著名的乐府诗歌。

词语解释

心急如火——心里急得像火烧一样,形容非常着急。

泪如雨下——眼泪像下雨一样地流。

痛不欲生——悲痛得不想活下去,形容悲伤到极点。

婆婆——丈夫的妈妈。

 *English Translation*

Lesson Two

Yuefu

Yuefu came into being in the Han Dynasty. The name "yuefu" is the name of the official conservatory to minister songs and dances. It collected from the grassroots folksongs that were called Yuefu Folksongs. The songs embrace a rich content of social life, and the language is plain and vivid. Among these songs, the most popular ones are *Southeast the Lonesome Peacock Flies* of the late Eastern Han Dynasty and *The Ballad of Mulan* of the Northern and Southern Dynasties. Afterwards, some poets followed the style of yuefu and produced many yuefu poems.

Southeast the Lonesome Peacock Flies

Southeast the Lonesome Peacock Flies is the most excellent long narrative poem of the folksongs of Hanyuefu (Yuefu of the Han Dynasty). The poet is unknown. The poem, with its 340 and more lines, tells the tragic love story of the youths of Jiao Zhongqing and Liu Lanzhi. In the past hundreds of years, it has been circulated among the people and deeply moved the readers.

The poem starts with:

**Southeast the lonesome peacock flies,
From time to time she hesitates and wanders.**

A lonely peacock is flying in the sky, looking for its sweetheart here and there, not willing to fly away. The same story happens in human world. Liu Lanzhi is a pretty girl who is industrious, educated and reasonable. In the poem she says:

**At the age of thirteen, I learned to weave white silk.
At fourteen I knew how to make clothes.
At fifteen I could play the Konghou.
At sixteen I could recite classical works.**

Liu Lanzhi, seventeen years old, beautiful as an angel, is married to Jiao Zhongqing, a low ranking official. The two love each other dearly. Yet they can rarely meet because Jiao Zhongqing is always off on business. Alone at home, Lanzhi begins weaving before dawn, producing scores feet of cloth in three days. But her mother-in-law is not satisfied with her and often deliberately blames her for nothing. The poem says:

Since I married you at seventeen,
Always feeling miserable I have been.
Now that you work for the government all day long,
My love for you remains as strong.
Day after day I stay lonely without you,
The chances for us to meet are few.
I begin working with the day's first light,
Weaving at the loom till midnight.
I can weave scores feet of cloth in three days,
Yet your mother blames me for no reasons always.

    She can no longer endure the pressure from her mother-in-law and says: Now that Mother-in-law does not like me, please send me to my mother's home. Knowing this, Jiao Zhongqing, knelling, pleads with his mother saying that Lanzhi has nothing to blame, why she should be driven away. He continues: If Mother does not want to have her here and she must leave, I would definitely not marry any other girl. His mother gets furious on his words and yells to him: How dare you refuse me! How could you possibly speak for Liu Lanzhi?

    Helpless and tearing, Jiao Zhongqing sends Lanzhi to her mother's home. When parting, Jiao Zhongqing says that Lanzhi's leaving is but a short one and he will surely bring her home in near future. Lanzhi, too, vows to heaven to wait for Jiao Zhongqing.

    But things happen beyond their expectation. Not long after Lanzhi comes home, the county magistrate, knowing that Lanzhi is pretty and kind, asks Lanzhi to marry his son. When Mother asked if she agrees or not, Lanzhi says with tears:

When I left for home, Zhongqing again and again
Advised me devoted I should remain.
We vowed to each other
Never to endure departure.

    Mother knows that Lanzhi is still waiting for Jiao Zhongqing and she sends the runner back. Not long after that, the prefect asks Lanzhi to marry his son and she again refuses. But her brother becomes impatient. To him, the prefect's son is not only wealthy, but also with high position. It is a glorious thing for Lanzhi to marry him. Why should she wait for Jiao Zhongqing? But finally Lanzhi's brother forces her to accept the court.

    When Jiao Zhongqing learns the news, he is deeply worried and rushes back on horse to see Lanzhi. They both cry bitterly when they meet. To them, although the universe is as big as it is, there is not even one inch of land for them to stay on. Therefore they both promise to die and reunite under the ground since they can not be husband and wife when they are alive.

    After their departure, the prefect's escorting team of several hundred strong comes and takes Lanzhi away. At the night of the newly marriage, Lanzhi woefully ends her life in a pond. Jiao Zhongqing, too, hangs himself when he gets the news. The poem goes:

My life ends today,
My soul will wander but my body will stay.
Skirt lifted, barefooted, she waded with a strong will
Into the pond the water of which was clear and still.
When Zhongqing learned the grievous information,
He was sure Lanzhi's death was their eternal separation.
Lingering about under the courtyard tree thick and tall,
He hanged himself on its southeast brand, once and for all.
With the demand of both families — a joint funeral,
The lovers' tomb now stands on Mount Huashan's side after burial.
Pines and cypresses are planted at its east and west,
And wutong trees grow at its right and left.
The boughs and branches intertwine like the lovers' arms,
With foliage embracing one another, the world is full of charms.
Among the greens reside two birds, pretty and young,
They call themselves with the name of love — Yuanyang.
The two sing to each other with heads holding high everyday,
Their songs echo in the air till morning's first ray.

After Liu Lanzhi and Jiao Zhongqing's death, the two families bury them in one tomb. They plant pines trees and wutong trees by the grave. When the trees grow into a forest, their souls turn into two birds named Yuanyang – the symbol of love. They have never departed ever since.

The Song of a Roaming Son
[Tang] Meng Jiao

With thread and needle
My loving mother labored ceaselessly,
To make the garment for his son
Ready for traveling endlessly.

Every inch of the garment is durably made
So it'll never wear off and always fit well;
She is worried deeply in her heart for
At what time I might come home nobody can tell.

With rain and sunshine little grass grow healthy and tall,
But they can in no way return the blessing to nature.
So great and selfless is mother's love to me,
How can I in whatever way repay her in the future?

第三课

唐 诗（一）

　　唐代的诗歌是中国古代诗歌的高峰。那时诗人多达两千，所写的诗歌近五万首。这些诗歌内容丰富，真实、生动地反映了唐代人民的生活。唐诗的形式多种多样，不仅有句式自由的古体诗歌，也创造了句式固定整齐的新诗体，这就是律诗和绝句。律诗全诗共八句，每句五字的，称五言律诗；每句七字的，称七言律诗。绝句全诗共四句，每句五字的，称五言绝句；每句七字的，称七言绝句。律诗和绝句对音韵和格律的要求非常严格，使诗歌不但看起来形式工整、优美，而且读起来音韵也很优美、动听。唐代最著名的诗人有李白、杜甫(fǔ)和白居易等。

登 鹳(guàn) 雀 楼
（五言绝句）

［唐］王之涣

白日依山尽，
黄河入海流。
欲穷千里目，
更上一层楼。

【注释】

鹳雀楼：在山西省永济县，位于黄河边，是唐代的名胜。

依：依傍；紧挨着。(āi)

尽：完；到头；全部。这里指太阳落山。

欲：想要；希望；需要；将要。

穷：用尽。

更：再。

【诗文讲解】

诗的前两句描写作者从鹳雀楼远望的壮观景象：傍晚，太阳在起伏的群山中慢慢落下。滚滚的黄河水向远方奔流而去。这高山大河的壮美画面，令诗人感叹。随着一步步登上楼的高层，诗人的视线越来越远，眼界越来越开阔，使他感悟到一个哲理：只有站得更高，才能看得更远。

第三课

望庐山瀑布
（七言绝句）

［唐］李白

日照香炉生紫烟，
遥看瀑布挂前川。
飞流直下三千尺，
疑是银河落九天。

【注释】

庐山：中国名山，在江西省。

香炉：指庐山的香炉峰。

九天：指天，"九"字形容天高到极点。

【诗文讲解】

作者用夸张的手法写出了庐山瀑布的壮丽景色：清晨，阳光照着香炉峰，紫云袅(niǎo)袅。从远处看去，瀑布高高地挂在石壁上。瀑布从高山顶上飞流直下，就好像是九重天上的银河落了下来。

春 望
（五言律诗）

［唐］杜甫

国破山河在，城春草木深。

感时花溅泪，恨别鸟惊心。

烽火连三月，家书抵万金。

白头搔更短，浑欲不胜簪(zān)。

【注释】

国破：指京城长安被叛军攻破。

烽火：古代边防报警的烟火；这里指战争。

家书：家信。

抵：相当于。

短：少，缺。

浑：全；这里的意思是简直。

簪：用来别住头发的一种首饰。

【诗文讲解】

长安城被攻破了，可是山河还在。春天来了，长安城野草丛生。与亲人分隔的痛苦使诗人见花落泪，听到鸟的叫声也觉得惊心。战乱已经连续三个月了，一封家信抵得上万两黄金哪！白发越搔越少，简直连簪子都插不住了。

诗人写这首诗时，正当安史之乱①，他身陷叛军占领下的长安城。山河破碎，家人离散，满目荒凉的景象，使诗人感叹战乱给国家和人民带来的苦难，也让他产生了对亲人强烈的思念之情。

作者简介

杜甫（712—770），唐代伟大的现实主义诗人，生活在唐朝由强盛走向衰亡的时期。他经历了国家的战乱，体会到了人民生活的痛苦。杜甫的诗歌真实地反映了那个动乱时代的社会生活。他一生写了大量诗歌，现存的有一千四百多首，被称为"诗圣"。

---

① 安史之乱——唐朝安禄山、史思明发动的叛乱。

生词

gù dìng 固定	fixed	lóu 楼	a storied building
yīn yùn 音韵	rhyme and tone (of Chinese characters)	yì céng 一层	one floor
gé lǜ 格律	rules and forms (of classical poetic composition)	kāi kuò 开阔	open; wide
yán gé 严格	strict; rigid	lú shān 庐山	Lushan Mountain
gōng zhěng 工整	neat and orderly	pù bù 瀑布	waterfall
dòng tīng 动听	pleasant to listen to	fēng huǒ 烽火	beacon fire
dēng 登	ascend; mount	sāo 搔	scratch

背诵并默写

《登鹳雀楼》和《望庐山瀑布》（"鹳"字可以用拼音）

比一比

瀑（瀑布）/ 爆（爆炸）

烽（烽火）/ 峰（山峰）

层 { 一层 / 地层 }

楼（高楼）/ 搂（搂着）

登（登山）/ 瞪（瞪眼）

律 { 格律 / 纪律 }

回答问题

1. 中国古代诗歌的高峰是什么时候？

2. 唐代创造了哪两种新诗体？

3. 唐代最著名的诗人有谁？请至少说出三位诗人。

4. 选做题："日照香炉生紫烟，遥看瀑布挂前川。飞流直下三千尺，疑是银河落九天。"其中哪一句采用了夸张的想象？

朗读

唐诗三首

Lesson Three

Tang Poems （Part I）

    The poems of the Tang Dynasty mark the highlights of the ancient Chinese poetry. During that period, about 2,000 poets produced almost 50,000 poems. The Tang poems, with their rich contents, reflect the life of the Tang people truly and expressively. The style of Tang poems varies a great deal, including the old style, the sentences structure of which are rather free, and newly created styles, the sentence structures of which are strictly fixed as lushi and jueju. A lushi is a poem of eight lines. If one line of which contains five characters, it is called wuyanlushi (pentasyllabic regulated verse). If one line of which contains seven characters, it is called qiyanlushi (heptasyllabic regulated verse). There are four lines in a jueju. If one line of which contains five characters, it is called wuyanjueju (pentasyllabic quatrain). If seven characters, it is a qiyanjueju (heptasyllabic quatrain). Both lushi and jueju are composed with strict tonal patterns and rhyme schemes so that they not only look neat and graceful, but also read pleasant to ears. The famous poets of the Tang Dynasty include Li Bai, Du Fu and Bai Juyi, etc.

Ascending the Stork Tower
(a wuyanjueju)
[Tang] Wang Zhihuan

Behind the mountains is the setting sun,
To the East Sea we see the Yellow River run.
If you wish to get a better view of the world,
To climb a higher story is all to be done.

The View of the Lushan Waterfall
(a qiyanjueju)
[Tang] Li Bai

Sunlight has put Xianglu Peak in purplish haze,
From far away I attentively gaze.
On a steep a water-fall hanging,
Down from a 3,000-foot height, roaring;
As if it has fallen into sight right away,
From the Ninth Heaven's Milky Way.

The Spring Prospect
(a wuyanlüshi)
[Tang] Du Fu

My country has been destroyed,
But mountains and rivers remain;
When spring arrives as expected,
Weeds and trees grow all the same.

The wilderness blooms without delay.
This brings up my tears sad,
Departed have I and my family for long,
Even the chirps of birds frighten me mad.

For three months the savage war continues,
Allowing no mails for people to receive and hold;
A letter from home coming through iron and blood,
Is so dear no one'd swap for ten thousand in gold.

My hair is turning scarce and white,
And thinner still when scratched by hand;
When I try to put a hairpin on,
Without help it can not stand.

第四课

唐 诗（二）

将(qiāng)进酒

[唐] 李白

君不见，黄河之水天上来，

奔流到海不复回。

君不见，高堂明镜悲白发，

朝如青丝暮成雪。

人生得意须尽欢，

莫使金樽(zūn)空对月。

天生我材必有用，

千金散尽还复来。

烹羊宰牛且为乐，

会须一饮三百杯。

岑(cén)夫子，丹丘生，

将进酒，杯莫停。

与君歌一曲,

请君为我倾耳听。

钟鼓馔玉何足贵,

但愿长醉不愿醒。

古来圣贤皆寂寞,

惟有饮者留其名。

陈王昔时宴平乐,

斗酒十千恣欢谑。

主人何为言少钱,

径须沽取对君酌。

五花马,千金裘,

呼儿将出换美酒,

与尔同销万古愁。

【注释】

将进酒:将,念作qiāng,请;将进酒,请喝酒。

樽:古代盛酒的器具,酒杯。

烹:煮。

岑夫子、丹丘生:指李白的两个朋友。

倾耳听:倾,歪倒;倾耳听,用力倾听,这里指仔细听。

钟鼓:鸣钟击鼓作乐,这里指富贵人家的音乐。

馔玉:馔,饮食;玉,像玉一样美好;馔玉,珍美如玉的饮食。

圣贤:指品格高尚、才智过人的人。

陈王:即曹植。

昔时:从前。

宴平乐:"平乐"为一道观(guàn)名;曹植《名都篇》中有"归来宴平乐,美酒斗十千"的诗句。

恣:任意。

谑:开玩笑。

沽:买。

酌：斟酒；饮酒。zhēn

将出：将，念作jiāng，拿。

尔：你。

销：除去，消除。

【诗文讲解】

这首诗是在李白初入京城，失意而归，与朋友相会时写下的一首"劝酒歌"。

难道你没有看见黄河之水从高天奔流而下，东入大海，如时光奔流不回？难道你没有看见镜中的黑发，转眼间已变为雪白，是多么令人伤悲！然而，人生并不是一杯苦酒，还是和朋友们痛快地饮酒谈笑吧，不要让精美的酒杯空对明月。"天生我材必有用"，千金散尽还会有的。功名富贵，不过是过眼烟云。朝廷让人失望，金钱、物品都不必珍惜，只有美酒可以消愁。tíng

这首诗虽然流露出诗人对自己得不到重用的感叹，但还是表达了豪放、乐观的情怀，是一部不可多得的好作品，是李白的代表作之一。

作者简介

李白（701—762），唐代最伟大的浪漫主义诗人。他的诗歌想象力惊人，风格豪放，使人过目难忘。李白常用高度夸张的手法来表达强烈的感情。他一生写了很多诗歌，现存的有一千多首，被称为"诗仙"。

生词

mò 莫	not; don't		yàn 宴	banquet
pēng 烹	cook		jìng zhí 径(直)	straight; directly
qīng tīng 倾听	listen attentively		gū 沽	buy
shèng xián 圣贤	sages and men of virtue		zhuó 酌	drink
jì mò 寂寞	lonesome; lonely		qiú 裘	fur coat
xī shí 昔时	the past		chóu 愁	worry; distress

背诵并默写

《将进酒》的前八句

比一比

宴 { 宴会 / 宴请 }　　圣 { 圣贤 / 圣人 }　　倾 { 倾倒 / 倾听 }

根据课文选择正确答案

1. 《将进酒》的作者是_____。

   A. 孟郊　　　　B. 杜甫　　　　C. 李白

 中国诗歌欣赏

2. "君不见黄河之水天上来，奔流到海不复回"

比喻_____。

 A.黄河的源头太高 B.河水不会倒流 C.时光飞快过去

3. "君不见高堂明镜悲白发，朝如青丝暮成雪"

比喻_____。

 A.头发白得早   B.人生短暂   C.镜子不好

4. "天生我材必有用，千金散尽还复来"

表达了李白_____的心情。

 A.自信、乐观   B.痛恨   C.悲伤

 译文 English Translation

Lesson Four

Tang Poems (Part II)

Let's Drink More
[Tang] Li Bai

Don't you see the Yellow River roaring from the sky,
Surging to the East Sea and never coming back?
Don't you see the mirror in the hall lamenting your hair,
Now snowy white but in the morning pitch-black?
Elate, you should drink to your full without stop, alas!
Never let the moon accompany your empty wine glass.

We are born talents
And we must be useful in some way.
A thousand taels of gold may be spent,
But they can be earned again someday.
Slaughter a cow and cook a lamb,
We enjoy ourselves freely,
After three hundred glasses of wine,
Clear-minded we remain joyfully.
Cen and Qiu, my dear friends,
Fill you glass and bottom up.
I invite you to more wine,
Glass after glass let's drink, don't stop!
I will now sing a song for you,
Please listen to me, the chances are few.
Excellent food and beautiful music,
Matter not to us whatever.
All I wish is to stay drunk,
Sober will we become never.
From ancient time the masterminds
Were all well forgotten;
Only those heavy drinkers whose names
Are still in people's mind written.
Cao Zhi in his poem mentions
His feast in Ping'le a Taoist temple of that time,
Where ten thousand taels of gold
Can only buy one cask of wine.
The host needs not complain about our lack of money,
To drink with you I would surely sell everything worthy.
I would sell my dappled horse
And my dear fur coat you will rarely find,
With the money we can buy more beautiful wine,
So that all the sorrows may slip from our mind.

第五课

唐 诗（三）

卖 炭 翁

［唐］白居易

卖炭翁，

伐薪烧炭南山中。

满面尘灰烟火色，

两鬓苍苍十指黑。（hè）

卖炭得钱何所营？

身上衣裳口中食。

可怜身上衣正单，

心忧炭贱愿天寒。

夜来城外一尺雪，

晓驾炭车辗冰辙。（zhé）

牛困人饥日已高，

市南门外泥中歇。

翩翩两骑来是谁？（jì）

黄衣使者白衫儿。
手把文书口称敕(chì)，
回车叱牛牵向北。
一车炭，千余斤，
宫使驱将惜不得！
半匹红纱一丈绫，
系向牛头充炭值。

【注释】

伐薪烧炭：砍柴，将木柴烧成炭。

两鬓苍苍：耳朵前边的头发都白了。

何所营：做什么用？

衣正单：穿的衣服很单薄。

心忧炭贱：担心木炭的价钱太低。

辗冰辙：车轮压在路面的冰雪上，辗出车辙。

牛困人饥：牛累了，人饿了。

敕(zhào)：帝王的命令，诏书。

叱：大声责骂。

千余斤：一千多斤。

宫使驱将惜不得：宫里的人拿走了，心疼也没办法。

充炭值：值，价值；算作买炭的钱。

作者简介

白居易（772—846），唐代著名诗人。父亲是个小官。父亲去世后，家庭生活困苦，因此白居易比较了解社会现实生活。他一生留下的诗作将近三千首，作品通俗易懂，反映了人民生活的疾苦，表达了诗人的同情之心。相传他写好诗以后，都要先读给不识字的老妈妈听，老妈妈听懂了，他才拿出去，因此他的诗在社会上流传很广。

生词

fá 伐	fell; chop		piān piān 翩翩	elegant; trippingly
xīn 薪	firewood		chì 叱	shout at
liǎng bìn 两鬓	the temples		qiān 牵	lead (by holding the halter)
yōu 忧	worry		qū 驱	drive; expel
jiàn 贱	cheap		shā 纱	gauze
jià chē 驾车	draw a cart		líng 绫	damask silk
niǎn 辗	crush		jì 系	fasten; tie
jī 饥	hungry		jià zhí （价）值	price; value
xiē 歇	take a rest			

背诵并默写

《卖炭翁》前八句

中国诗歌欣赏

比一比

$$\begin{cases} 伐（伐木）\\ 代（古代）\end{cases} \begin{cases} 饥（饥饿）\\ 几（几个）\end{cases} 营\begin{cases} 营养\\ 经营\end{cases}$$

$$\begin{cases} 薪（薪水）\\ 新（新年）\end{cases} \begin{cases} 纱（纱布）\\ 沙（沙土）\end{cases} 惜\begin{cases} 可惜\\ 爱惜\end{cases}$$

字词运用

驾车

下雨天驾车，要特别注意安全。

驾车时最好不要打手机。

价值

这辆高级跑车价值90,000美元。

这台手提电脑价值8,000元。

回答问题

1. 卖炭翁的工作辛苦不辛苦？

2. 他准备用卖炭的钱来做什么？

3. 天那么冷，卖炭翁衣服穿得暖和吗？

4. 卖炭翁的衣服穿得很单薄，为什么他还希望天气寒冷呢？

5. 宫使给卖炭翁很少的东西就拿走一大车炭，公平不公平？

Lesson Five

Tang Poems (Part III)

The Charcoal Vender
[Tang] Bai Juyi

The old charcoal vender in Mount Nanshan,
Hews wood and makes charcoal.
Covered by dust and smoked by heat,
His face looks dark and dirty and all.
Temples grey, fingers black,
Hard life has bent his back.
Daily clothes and daily foods
Are all he's for to sell his goods.
In thin coat he cannot but shiver,
But he wants it colder, for the price may be higher.
One foot deep the night's snow has fallen,
Covering all outside the city wall olden.
With his ox cart setting off before the first glow,
Wheels leaving ruts clear in dazzling snow.
Ox tired, driver hungry, the sun has risen high,
Outside the south gate in the mud a rest they can't deny.
Dressed in yellow and white garments,
Two horse riders are coming swiftly around.
With orders from His Majesty, documents of the Court,
The Emperor's men force the cart and ox northbound.
A thousand catties and more
The cartload of charcoal must weigh.
But in face of the emperor's power and bully,
It's unfair, but submission is the only way,
They put on the ox horn half a bolt of red silk
And bits of satin on His Majesty's behalf,
As payment of the cartload of charcoal,
But it does not cover the cost, not even half.

第六课

宋　词（一）

　　"词"早在唐代就已经有了，但是到了宋代，词才真正流行起来。词按不同的格式填写，句子有长有短，更有表现力。《全宋词》一书中，收集了一千三百多人的两万多首词。词的创作到宋代达到了高峰，最有名的词作者有苏轼(shì)、陆游等。

念奴娇·赤壁怀古①

[北宋]苏轼

大江东去，
浪淘尽、
千古风流人物。
故垒西边，
人道是、
三国周郎赤壁。

---

① 念奴娇·赤壁怀古——念奴娇是一个词牌名（词调的名称），《赤壁怀古》是诗词的题目。赤壁，地名，在今中国湖北省。

乱石穿空,

惊涛拍岸,

卷(juǎn)起千堆雪。

江山如画,

一时多少豪杰!

遥想公瑾当年,

小乔初嫁了,

雄姿英发。

羽扇纶巾,

谈笑间、

强虏①灰飞烟灭。

故国神游,

多情应笑我,

早生华发。

人生如梦,

一樽(zūn)还酹(lèi)江月。

---

① 在有的版本中"强虏"也作"樯橹(qiáng lǔ)"。

【注释】

怀古：追念古代的事情。

风流人物：这里指英雄人物。

故垒：古代军营的墙壁或工事。

周郎（yú）：指周瑜。

公瑾：周瑜的字。

雄姿：英武的样子。

小乔：三国时期最有名的美人之一。

纶巾：古代配有青丝带的头巾。

强虏：强大的敌人。

酹：把酒洒在地上，表示纪念。

【诗文讲解】

这是苏轼游赤壁时写下的一首名作。

波澜（lán）壮阔的历史，就像滚滚东流的长江水，后浪推前浪，永不停息。千百年来，在中华大地上发生了多少惊天动地的事件，涌现出多少气势非凡的英雄。江岸上古迹的西边，听说是三国时周瑜大破曹军的赤壁古战场。那里，巨石高耸（sǒng），直入云间，汹涌的江水拍打着岸边，层层浪花像一堆堆白雪。如此美好的江山，哺（bǔ）育出多少英雄豪杰！

回想周瑜当年，年轻、英武。美丽的小乔嫁给了他。他与才智过人的诸葛亮在从容的谈笑中，制定出了打败曹军的计划，一把火烧得曹军战船灰飞烟灭，建立了赫（hè）赫战功。

48

重游古战场，诗人笑自己对历史太动情了，以致早早地白了头发。缅(miǎn)怀古人，对照自己，诗人感伤自己年纪老大还没有建功立业，不由感叹道：人生短暂，真像一场梦啊！暂且举起酒杯，将酒倒入江中，来祭(jì)月亮吧！

作者简介

苏轼（1037—1101）是北宋时期的大文学家、书法家、画家，在中国文学史上占有重要地位。在诗歌创作方面，他开创了豪放词派，对后世有很大的影响。《念奴娇·赤壁怀古》是千古传诵的杰作，也是苏轼的代表作之一。后人用这个词调的时候，有的就用"大江东去"或"酹江月"来代替"念奴娇"，由此可见这首词的名气和影响有多大！

生词

奴 nú	slave	姿 zī	appearance; carriage
淘 táo	wash	纶巾 guān jīn	silk hood
豪杰 háo jié	hero	虏 lǔ	enemy; captive
公瑾 gōng jǐn	Gongjin (*another name of Zhou Yu*)		

默写

《念奴娇·赤壁怀古》前十一行

比一比

$$\begin{cases} 嫁（出嫁）\\ 家（家庭） \end{cases} \qquad 杰\begin{cases} 豪杰\\ 杰出 \end{cases}$$

$$\begin{cases} 豪（富豪）\\ 毫（毫毛） \end{cases} \qquad 格\begin{cases} 格式\\ 格子 \end{cases}$$

多音字

卷 juǎn

风卷着乌云。

岸边停放的小船，被海浪卷走了。

卷 juàn

《本草纲目》全书共52卷。

老师拿着考卷走进教室。

根据课文选择正确答案

1. 《念奴娇·赤壁怀古》的作者是_____。

   A.李白　　　　　B.杜甫　　　　　C.苏轼

2. 《念奴娇·赤壁怀古》是_____。

   A.诗　　　　　　B.词　　　　　　C.楚辞

3. 苏轼是_____的大文学家。

   A.宋朝　　　　　B.战国　　　　　C.唐朝

词语解释

江山——江河和山岭，常用来指国家。

背诵

《念奴娇·赤壁怀古》

Lesson Six

Song Ci (Part I)

  Ci (poetry in ci form or ci poetry) existed as early as in the Tang Dynasty, but it became popular in the Song Dynasty. Ci is written strictly according to specific tonal patterns. The lines can be long or short so that they can convey the poet's feelings more powerfully. *A Complete Collection of Song Ci* contains more than 20,000 ci by more than 1,300 poets. Ci reached its peak in the Song Dynasty. The most famous ci poets include Su Shi and Lu You, etc.

Thinking Back on the Red Cliff
to the tonal pattern of *Niannujiao*
[Northern Song] Su Shi

The great Yangtze surges east,
Washing away
All the heroic men in the past thousands of years.
West of the ancient fortress – they say –
Is the Red Cliff where the glorious victories of
Zhou Yu of the Three Kingdoms' time stay.
Rugged steeps scrape the sky,
Mountainous waves rip the shores,
Churning thousands of snow mounds with roars.
Among these mountains and rivers beautiful as paintings,
Countless heroes have gained their doings!

We think of Gongjin of those years –
When he just married Qiao the younger –
With plumed fan and silk hood,
Showing a heroic and vigorous posture.
He talked and laughed
While in flames and smoke o'er his foes he triumphed.
When visiting this ancient battlefield sentimentally,
So impressed and moved I see my hair turned grey untimely.
Although life is like a dream passing soon,
Still I toast to the River and the Moon!

第七课

宋 词（二）

钗 头 凤[①]

[南宋]陆游

红酥手，黄縢(téng)酒。

满城春色宫墙柳。

东风恶，欢情薄，

一怀愁绪，几年离索。

错！错！错！

春如旧，人空瘦，

泪痕红浥(yì)鲛(jiāo)绡(xiāo)透。

桃花落，闲池阁，

山盟虽在，锦书难托。

莫！莫！莫！

[①] 钗头凤——词牌名。

中国诗歌欣赏

【注释】

红酥手：女人红润细嫩（nèn）的手。

黄縢酒：古代的一种酒。

东风：这里比喻诗人的母亲。

欢情薄：美满的爱情遭到破坏。

一怀愁绪：满心的愁苦。

离索：别离。

春如旧，人空瘦：春天还是如期而至，但心上人已憔悴（qiáo cuì）不堪（kān）。

泪痕红浥鲛绡透：浥，沾湿；鲛绡，手帕（pà）、丝巾；泪水滴落，湿透了丝帕。

桃花落，闲池阁：春天将尽，桃花散落，池水边楼阁上，再没有人来约会游玩了。

山盟虽在，锦书难托：原来立下的海誓山盟还在心中，但是现在两人相互间连信都不能写了。

【诗文讲解】

早年，陆游曾娶唐琬(wǎn)为妻，词的开头就追忆了唐琬的美丽和以前两人之间幸福美满的爱情生活。但是因为婆婆不喜欢唐琬，活活把他们分开了。几年后的一个春天，陆游在家乡的沈(shěn)园又碰到已嫁给别人的唐琬，心中悲伤，于是提笔在沈园的墙壁上写下了这首词，表达了美满爱情被破坏以后深深的痛苦。

作者简介

陆游（1125—1210），南宋爱国诗人。他生活的时代，正是南宋不断受到金国入侵(qīn)的时代。陆游也做过官，坚决主张抗金。他一生留下九千多首诗，其中许多诗反映了他抗金爱国的热情。

钗 头 凤

［南宋］唐琬

世情薄，人情恶，

雨送黄昏花易落。

晓风干，泪痕残，

欲笺心事,独语斜阑。
难!难!难!

人成各,今非昨,
病魂常似秋千索。
角声寒,夜阑珊,
怕人寻问,咽泪装欢。
瞒!瞒!瞒!

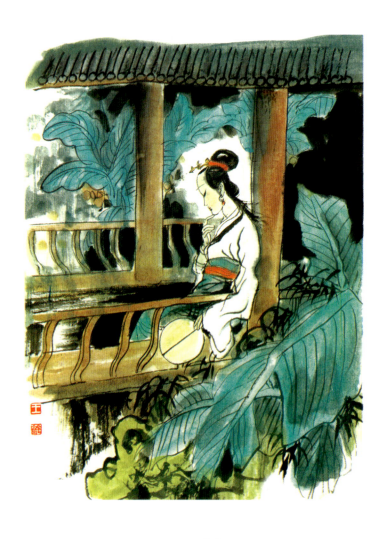

【注释】

晓风：晨风。

泪痕残：脸上留下眼泪的痕迹。

欲笺心事：想要写信说说心事。

斜阑：这里"阑"同"栏"。斜阑，斜靠着栏杆。

人成各，今非昨：现在不比以前，她与陆游已成为互不相干的两个人了。

秋千索：秋千的绳子。

角声寒：号角声凄凉。

夜阑珊：阑珊，将尽；夜阑珊，黑夜快要过去了。

【诗文讲解】

对唐琬来说，世间的人情太冷、太薄。她与陆游这对恩爱夫妻被婆婆活活拆散。她觉得自己就像在黄昏中被风雨吹打的花，满身是伤。一夜夜的泪水，一次次地被晨风吹干，满心的痛苦又能向谁诉说？只能独自靠着栏杆叹息："难！难！难！"

唐琬感到自己的命运就像秋千上的绳子，飘飘荡荡，不能自主。更不幸的是唐琬改嫁后，连表达悲苦的自由都没有了。长夜无眠，听着凄凉的号角声，让人心碎，直到天明，又"怕人寻问，咽泪装欢"，只能"瞒！瞒！瞒！"

据说唐琬作此词后不久就去世了。这首词表达了她对封建礼法的不满和她内心的巨大痛苦。如泣如诉，真切感人。

生词

chāi 钗	an ornament formerly worn by women	lèi hén 泪痕	tear stains
sū 酥	soft; limp; crisp	cán 残	remaining
(qíng) xù (情)绪	mood	jiān 笺	writing paper
shān méng (hǎi shì) 山盟(海誓)	a solemn pledge of love	xié 斜	lean; incline
jǐn 锦	brocade	lán 阑	railing
tuō 托	entrust	yàn 咽	swallow

默写

《钗头凤》(陆游)前五行(生字可以用汉语拼音)

字词运用

情绪

比赛之前,队员们情绪高涨,信心十足。

根据课文选择正确答案

1. 陆游是_____的人。

   A.汉朝　　　　　B.唐朝　　　　　C.宋朝

2. 陆游《钗头凤》是一首_____。

   A.诗　　　　　　B.词　　　　　　C.楚辞

3. "春如旧，人空瘦"意思是_____。

   A.春天如期而至，但心上人已憔悴不堪

   B.春天来了，人很瘦

词语解释

山盟海誓——男女相爱立下的誓言和盟约，表示爱情要像山和海那样永远不变。

背诵

《钗头凤》（陆游）

Lesson Seven

Song Ci (Part II)

To the Tonal Pattern of *Chaitoufeng*
[Southern Song] Lu You

So soft and pink are your hands,
So savory and mellow is the wine.
Willow twigs hang o'er the palace wall,
Reporting the arrival of spring time.
Merciless mother destroyed our marriage life,
Our happiness will hence return never.
Ever since our departure many years have passed,
My sorrow and bitterness will last for ever.
All this is Wrong! Wrong! Wrong!

Spring has come again as usual,
Grievance has turned you weak and lean.
Your silk clothes are wet all through,
'Cause tears run down like a stream.
Peach flower petals falling, spring leaving,
Pond and pavilion remain, but without thee.
Though our vow for love still lingers in the air,
I can't send letters to you, nor you to me.
Let it not happen again. No! No! No!

To the Tonal Pattern of *Chaitoufeng*
[Southern Song] Tang Wan

Cruel is the world,
Cold is people's heart.
Evening gusts and rain
Forcing petals to fall apart.
Morning breeze dried my eyes,
Trace of weeping almost disappears.
I'm eager to speak out my mind, but I can only
Lean on the fence talking to myself in tears.
Life is really Hard! Hard! Hard!

The two of us have separated totally,
Today has nothing to do with yesterday.
The sick body hangs on feebly,
Like the ropes of a swing-weakly sway.
Desolating is the sound of bugles,
Sleepless is the night breaking.
For fear of being asked about the truth,
I have to keep to my own mind everything.
My real world? Hide! Hide! Hide!

第八课

宋　词（三）

满江红① · 写怀

［南宋］岳飞

怒发冲冠，

凭阑处、

潇潇雨歇。

抬望眼、

仰天长啸，

壮怀激烈。

三十功名尘与土，

八千里路云和月。

莫等闲、

白了少年头，

空悲切。

---

① 满江红——词牌名。

靖(jìng)康耻,

犹未雪。

臣子恨,

何时灭。

驾长车、

踏破贺兰山缺。

壮志饥餐胡虏肉,

笑谈渴饮匈奴血。

待从头、

收拾旧山河,

朝天阙。

【注释】

凭阑处：靠着栏杆站立。

潇潇：雨声。

啸：这里指长声喊叫。

壮怀激烈：壮志在心中激荡。

等闲：随随便便；轻易。

白了少年头：青少年变成了白发老人。

空悲切：一事无成而伤心悲哀。

靖康耻：指靖康元年（1126年）金军攻下宋朝首都，第二年又掳走宋朝皇帝及贵族大臣等三千多人，北宋从此灭亡的事件。

犹未雪：（耻辱）还没洗掉。

贺兰山缺：贺兰山，山名，在中国西北。缺，缺口，这里指山口。

胡虏：外敌，这里指金国人。

匈奴：这里指中国北方、西北地区其他的民族，主要指金国人。

朝天阙：阙，皇宫门前两边的瞭望楼，这里指皇宫；朝天阙，朝见皇帝。

【诗文讲解】

潇潇的细雨停了，岳飞站在高处的栏杆前，放眼远望，悲愤之情从心中涌出；抬起头向着长空大喊一声，誓死打败金兵收复国土的壮志在心中激荡。他回想一生转战万里抗敌报国的经历，更感到收复失地的紧迫，不能白白地浪费时间了。他想到靖康年的国耻至今未报，作为国

家的大臣，内心怎能平静呢？他要驾着战车直冲到贺兰山下，与敌人决一死战。等到打败了敌人的那一天，再重新修建可爱的家园。

这是一首千古杰作，表达了岳飞希望报仇雪恨、收复国土的悲壮心情。

作者简介

岳飞（1103—1142）南宋抗金名将。他主张抗金，带领南宋军队多次打败金军，收复失去的疆土。但是皇帝和大臣秦桧（huì）一心求和，将岳飞杀害。

生词

凭 píng	lean on	犹 yóu	still
潇潇 xiāo xiāo	whistling; drizzly	踏 tà	step on; tread
啸 xiào	roar; howl	匈奴 xiōng nú	Hun (*an ancient nationality in China*)
激烈 jī liè	violent; fierce	阙 què	watchtower on either side of a palace gate
耻 chǐ	shame		

默写

《满江红·写怀》前十一行

中国诗歌欣赏

根据课文选择正确答案

1. 《满江红·写怀》的作者是_____。

   A.岳飞　　　　B.李白　　　　C.苏轼

2. 岳飞是_____人。

   A.汉朝　　　　B.唐朝　　　　C.宋朝

3. 《满江红·写怀》表达了岳飞_____。

   A.希望报仇雪恨、收复国土的悲壮心情

   B.收回了国土的快乐心情

词语解释

怒发冲冠——头发直竖，把帽子都顶起来了。形容非常愤怒。

背诵

《满江红·写怀》

Lesson Eight

Song Ci （Part Ⅲ）

Expressing My Mind
to the tonal pattern of *Manjianghong*
[Southern Song] Yue Fei

Furious rage surging up to my helmet,
I lean on the railing.
It has stopped drizzling.
Lifting my eyes,
Towards the blue I give up to a roar,
I can not press my anger any more.
Nothing is thirty years of rank and reputations,
The moon and clouds see eight hundred leagues of expeditions.
Do not fool away your time.
Your hair turns white when you see in pain,
Grieve and regret you may but well in vain.

The national insult of Jingkang
Is still to be avenged wholly.
As to people's heartfelt hatred,
When shall it be cleared entirely?
We should ride our chariots of war,
To crush those foes in Helan Mountain's passes hiding.
Heroes! Eat the flesh of our foes when hungry.
Thirsty, drink Hun's blood chatting and laughing.
Let us begin immediately
Resuming our mountains and rivers.
When it is done, report to His Majesty.

第九课

古诗词二首

相见欢①

[南唐]李煜(yù)

无言独上西楼,

月如钩。

寂寞梧桐深院锁清秋。

剪不断,

理还乱,

是离愁。

别是一番滋味在心头。

【注释】

寂寞:孤单,冷清。

离愁:离别之苦。

---

① 相见欢——词牌名。

第九课

【诗文讲解】

　　独自登上西楼，静静地遥望茫茫夜空，一弯残月，照着庭院里的梧桐。这样寂寞、冷清的秋色也被锁在高墙深院中。然而，"锁"住的又何止是这满院的秋色？诗人心乱如麻："剪不断，理还乱，是离愁"。这种愁苦的滋味真是说不出地难受啊！

作者简介

　　李煜（937—978）是南唐最后一位皇帝，也是一位杰出的词人。他当皇帝时，南唐国力已经很弱，而宋强大起来。他一方面每年送金银等物给宋朝去讨好(tǎo)，另一方面又在生活上尽情享(xiǎng)乐。后来，南唐被宋所灭，他自己也成了囚(qiú)徒。这首《相见欢》就是他被囚禁之时写的。

中国诗歌欣赏

过零丁洋

[南宋] 文天祥(xiáng)

辛苦遭逢起一经,

干戈寥落四周星。

山河破碎风飘絮,

身世浮沉雨打萍。

惶恐滩头说惶恐，

零丁洋里叹零丁。

人生自古谁无死，

留取丹心照汗青。

【注释】

起一经：经，指四书五经；起一经，一生的艰辛就是从学习四书五经开始的。

四周星：四年光阴。

风飘絮：随风乱飘的柳絮。

身世：指人生的经历、遭遇。

惶恐滩：地名。

惶恐：惊慌、害怕。

零丁洋：地名。

零丁：同"伶仃"(líng dīng)；孤苦伶仃，没有依靠。

留取：留下。

丹心：红心，对祖国、民族忠诚的心。

汗青：史册(cè)，史书。

【诗文讲解】

小时苦读经书，立下保卫国家的远大志向。长大后做了官，正遇上元军入侵南宋。经过四年抗元战争，不幸被俘(fú)。眼看着祖国的山河被

敌军破坏得像四散的柳絮,自己的一生如同风雨中飘荡的浮萍。自古以来人都有一死,我要把这颗对祖国的忠心永远留在史册上。

作者在诗中回忆了自己抵抗元兵、保卫国家的艰难战斗,写出了山河破碎的痛苦,最后两句诗表现了作者视死如归的英雄气概。

作者简介

文天祥(1236—1283),南宋末年政治家和爱国诗人,生于江西,二十岁中状元(zhòng)。当元兵大举进攻南宋时,他组织军队抵抗,后来兵败被俘,1283年被杀害。囚禁中,文天祥写下了《过零丁洋》一诗。诗中"人生自古谁无死,留取丹心照汗青"一句成为千古绝句,传诵至今。

生词

钩 gōu	hook	滋味 zī wèi	taste; flavor
梧桐 wú tóng	Chinese parasol tree	零 líng	zero
锁 suǒ	lock up; lock	干戈 gān gē	arms
剪 jiǎn	cut; scissors	寥落 liáo luò	scattered; sparse
番 fān	a kind of; times	(浮)萍 fú píng	duckweed

背诵并默写

李煜的《相见欢》

文天祥的诗句"人生自古谁无死,留取丹心照汗青"

比一比

逢 { 相逢 / 重逢 }　　寥 { 寥落 / 寥寥无几 }　　浮 { 浮动 / 浮云 / 浮萍 }

恐 { 惶恐 / 恐怕 }　　寂 { 寂寞 / 寂静 }　　{ 番（一番）/ 翻（翻开）}

根据课文选择正确答案

1. 《相见欢》（无言独上西楼）的作者是_____。

　　A.李白　　　B.李煜

2. 李煜是南唐的_____。

　　A.皇帝　　　B.将军

3. "人生自古谁无死，留取丹心照汗青"是_____的诗句。

　　A.文天祥　　B.岳飞

朗读

《相见欢》

《过零丁洋》

Lesson Nine

Two Classical Poems

To the Tonal Pattern of *Xiangjianhuan*
[Southern Tang] Li Yu

Wordless I go up the western tower alone
The hooklike moon hanging,
Solitary wutong trees locked up in the deep courtyard
In this chilly and clear autumn standing.
No way to straighten it up,
Worse still if you try.
Grievous it is to part.
Unspeakable feelings in my heart lie.

Crossing the Lonesome Sea
[Southern Song] Wen Tianxiang

Studying hard the classics to protect motherland from childhood,
For four years I fought the invaders with might and main.
The war-torn country looks like willow catkin scattered,
Up and down my life equals to duckweed in wind and rain.
On Terrifying Beach I mentioned how I was terrified,
Crossing Lonesome Sea I felt lonesome and sighed.
It's true from the beginning all men must perish,
It's my loyalty in history I should like to establish.

第十课

现代诗二首

黄 河 颂

光未然

我站在高山之巅,
望黄河滚滚,
奔向东南。
金涛澎湃,
掀起万丈狂澜;
浊流宛转,
结成九曲连环;

从昆仑山下奔向黄海之边；

把中原大地劈成南北两面。

啊！黄河！

你是中华民族的摇篮！

五千年的古国文化，

从你这儿发源；

多少英雄的故事，

在你身边扮演！

啊！黄河！

你是伟大坚强，

像一个巨人出现在亚洲平原之上，

用你那英雄的体魄筑成我们民族的屏障。

啊！黄河！

你一泻万丈，

浩浩荡荡，

向南北两岸伸出千万条铁的臂膀。

我们民族的伟大精神，

将要在你的哺育下发扬滋长！

我们祖国的英雄儿女,

将要学习你的榜样,

像你一样的伟大坚强!

像你一样的伟大坚强!

【注释】

中原:指黄河中下游地区。

作品简介

《黄河大合唱》创作于抗日战争时期（1939年3月），由年轻的诗人光未然作词，冼(xiǎn)星海作曲。《黄河颂》是《黄河大合唱》中的一个乐章，也是中华民族的颂歌。它以中华民族的发源地之一——黄河为背景，歌颂了中华民族的古老、伟大和坚强，以及中华儿女对这片土地的深爱和永不屈服的精神。《黄河大合唱》气吞山河，具有鲜明的民族风格，是中国著名的交响音乐。

乡　愁

余光中

小时候

乡愁是一枚小小的邮票

我在这头

母亲在那头

长大后

乡愁是一张窄窄的船票

我在这头

新娘在那头

后来啊

乡愁是一方矮矮的坟墓

我在外头

母亲呵在里头

而现在

乡愁是一湾浅浅的海峡

我在这头

大陆在那头

作品简介

《乡愁》是台湾著名诗人余光中先生于1971年所写。诗歌抒发了他内心难以排解的思念故乡和亲人的感情。诗虽不长,却句句动人。

生词

sòng 颂	eulogy; ode		píng zhàng 屏障	protective screen
shān diān 山巅	the summit of a mountain		hào dàng 浩荡	vast and mighty
péng pài 澎湃	surge		bì bǎng 臂膀	arm and shoulder
xiān 掀	stir up; surge; uncover		bǔ yù 哺育	feed
kuáng lán 狂澜	raging waves		zī zhǎng 滋长	grow
wǎn zhuǎn 宛转	winding		bǎng yàng 榜样	model; example
wān qū (弯)曲	curved; bend		méi 枚	*measure word*
yáo lán 摇篮	cradle		yóu piào 邮票	stamp
bàn yǎn 扮演	play the part of		xīn niáng 新娘	bride
tǐ pò 体魄	physique and vigour		fén mù 坟墓	grave; tomb

听写

颂　掀　扮演　体魄　浩荡　臂膀　榜样　弯曲　邮票

*哺育　滋长　屏障

比一比

膀 { 臂膀 / 翅膀 }   滋 { 滋长 / 滋味 }   扮 { 扮演 / 打扮 }

字词运用

打扮　扮演

春节晚会上，同学们都打扮得很漂亮。

在这个戏中，哥哥扮演一个坏人的角色。

体魄

我们不但要学习好，而且要有强健的体魄。

跳伞运动员不但要有强健的体魄，而且头脑要清醒。

多音字

劈 pī
劈开 pī

劈 pǐ
劈柴 pǐ

曲 qū

曲 qǔ

弯曲 qū

歌曲 qǔ

回答问题

1. 阅读《黄河颂》最后七行，请想一想：诗人用黄河比喻了什么？（提示：A.不屈的民族精神　B.英雄的体魄）

2. 《乡愁》表达了诗人什么样的感情？（提示：A.思念邮票的感情　B.思念母亲的感情　C.思念故乡和亲人的感情）

词语解释

乡愁——思乡之愁。

海峡——这里指台湾海峡。

朗诵

《黄河颂》和《乡愁》

Lesson Ten

Two Contemporary Poems

Ode to the Yellow River
Guang Weiran

Standing on the peak of the mountain,
I watch the Yellow River
Rolling south-eastward forever.
In some parts raging torrents rise to the sky,
Mountainous billows and terrible waves swell high.
In some parts muddy currents wind,
Bends, interlinks and zigzag chains we find.
It runs from the foot of Kunlun Mountians
To the front of the Yellow Sea,
Cutting the Central Plains
Into halves – north and south as we see.
O, the Yellow River,
The cradle of the Chinese people!
Five-thousand years' civilization of this ancient nation
Takes root from your principle.
Countless heroic deeds
Happen by your body gracious.
O, the Yellow River,
Great , firm and tenacious
You're like a giant arising
On the plain of Asia.
With your mighty body
You build up the defense for China.
O, the Yellow River!
With unyielding vigor,
In formidable strength rushing
Toward south and north banks
Thousands of iron arms stretching.

Our lofty national spirit and essence,
Under your nurture
Is for ever in development and advance!
The courageous people of our motherland
Will follow your example and stand
As strong and firm as you!
As strong and firm as you!

Homesickness
Yu Guangzhong

When I was at my wee age,
My homesickness was that tiny stamp for postage.
I was at this end
Mother was at the other end.

When I became an adult
My homesickness was that strip of boat ticket.
I was at this end
My bride was at the other end.

With the passing of time
My homesickness was that square low shrine.
I was at its outside
But mother was inside.

Nowadays
My homesickness is that shallow strait.
I am on this side
The mainland is on the other side.

生字表(简)

1. piān fàn yìng bǐ ài jī chǔ sāo shū zhú fèn yǎn tì jīn suǒ
   篇 泛 映 彼 艾 基 础 骚 抒 逐 愤 掩 涕 禁 索
   zāo shuāi zòng
   遭 衰 粽

2. xù jiāo zhī chún pái huái lǚ qín lǎng sòng jià lì xián pò níng
   叙 焦 芝 纯 徘 徊 侣 勤 朗 诵 嫁 吏 嫌 迫 咛
   diào hún bǎi fù zàng yín jiāo cí huī
   吊 魂 柏 覆 葬 吟 郊 慈 晖

3. yùn lǜ dēng lóu lú pù fēng sāo
   韵 律 登 楼 庐 瀑 烽 搔

4. mò pēng qīng shèng xián jì mò xī yàn jìng gū zhuó qiú chóu
   莫 烹 倾 圣 贤 寂 寞 昔 宴 径 沽 酌 裘 愁

5. fá xīn bìn yōu jiàn jià niǎn jī xiē piān chì qiān qū shā líng
   伐 薪 鬓 忧 贱 驾 辗 饥 歇 翩 叱 牵 驱 纱 绫
   jì zhí
   系 值

6. nú táo háo jié jǐn zī guān lǔ
   奴 淘 豪 杰 瑾 姿 纶 虏

7. chāi sū xù méng jǐn tuō hén cán jiān xié lán yàn
   钗 酥 绪 盟 锦 托 痕 残 笺 斜 阑 咽

8. píng xiāo xiào liè chǐ yóu tà xiōng què
   凭 潇 啸 烈 耻 犹 踏 匈 阙

中国诗歌欣赏

9. 钩(gōu) 梧(wú) 桐(tóng) 锁(suǒ) 剪(jiǎn) 番(fān) 滋(zī) 零(líng) 戈(gē) 寥(liáo) 萍(píng)

10. 颂(sòng) 巅(diān) 澎(péng) 湃(pài) 掀(xiān) 澜(lán) 宛(wǎn) 曲(qū) 魄(pò) 屏(píng) 障(zhàng) 浩(hào) 臂(bì) 哺(bǔ) 榜(bǎng) 枚(méi) 邮(yóu) 票(piào) 坟(fén)

共计 140 个生字

生字表（繁）

1. 篇(piān) 泛(fàn) 映(yìng) 彼(bǐ) 艾(ài) 基(jī) 礎(chǔ) 騷(sāo) 抒(shū) 逐(zhú) 憤(fèn) 掩(yǎn) 涕(tì) 禁(jīn) 索(suǒ)
遭(zāo) 衰(shuāi) 粽(zòng)

2. 敘(xù) 焦(jiāo) 芝(zhī) 純(chún) 徘(pái) 徊(huái) 侶(lǚ) 勤(qín) 朗(lǎng) 誦(sòng) 嫁(jià) 吏(lì) 嫌(xián) 迫(pò) 嚀(níng)
弔(diào) 魂(hún) 柏(bǎi) 覆(fù) 葬(zàng) 吟(yín) 郊(jiāo) 慈(cí) 暉(huī)

3. 韻(yùn) 律(lǜ) 登(dēng) 樓(lóu) 廬(lú) 瀑(pù) 烽(fēng) 搔(sāo)

4. 莫(mò) 烹(pēng) 傾(qīng) 聖(shèng) 賢(xián) 寂(jì) 寞(mò) 昔(xī) 宴(yàn) 徑(jìng) 沽(gū) 酌(zhuó) 裘(qiú) 愁(chóu)

5. 伐(fá) 薪(xīn) 鬢(bìn) 憂(yōu) 賤(jiàn) 駕(jià) 輾(niǎn) 饑(jī) 歇(xiē) 翩(piān) 叱(chì) 牽(qiān) 驅(qū) 紗(shā) 綾(líng)
繫(jì) 值(zhí)

6. 奴(nú) 淘(táo) 豪(háo) 傑(jié) 瑾(jǐn) 姿(zī) 綸(guān) 虜(lǔ)

7. 釵(chāi) 酥(sū) 緒(xù) 盟(méng) 錦(jǐn) 託(tuō) 痕(hén) 殘(cán) 箋(jiān) 斜(xié) 闌(lán) 嚥(yàn)

8. 憑(píng) 瀟(xiāo) 嘯(xiào) 烈(liè) 恥(chǐ) 猶(yóu) 踏(tà) 匈(xiōng) 闕(què)

9.
gōu	wú	tóng	suǒ	jiǎn	fān	zī	líng	gē	liáo	píng
鈎	梧	桐	鎖	剪	番	滋	零	戈	寥	萍

10.
sòng	diān	péng	pài	xiān	lán	wǎn	qū	pò	píng	zhàng	hào	bì	bǔ
頌	巔	澎	湃	掀	瀾	宛	曲	魄	屏	障	浩	臂	哺

bǎng	méi	yóu	piào	fén
榜	枚	郵	票	墳

共計140個生字

生词表（简）

1. shōu jí　piān　guǎng fàn　fǎn yìng　yǐng xiǎng　bǐ　ài　xíng shì　làng màn　jī chǔ
   收集　篇　广泛　反映　影响　彼　艾　形式　浪漫　基础

   lí sāo　shū qíng　fàng zhú　bēi fèn　yǎn tì　jīn bu zhù　qiú suǒ　zhuī qiú　lǐ xiǎng
   离骚　抒情　放逐　悲愤　掩涕　禁不住　求索　追求　理想

   zāo yù　guì zú　mìng yùn　shuāi luò　jì niàn　zòng zi
   遭遇　贵族　命运　衰落　纪念　粽子

2. xù shì　liú lán zhī　chún zhēn　bēi jù　pái huái　bàn lǚ　qín láo　lǎng sòng　jià
   叙事　刘兰芝　纯真　悲剧　徘徊　伴侣　勤劳　（朗）诵　嫁

   fǔ lì　wéi nán　xián　bī pò　dīng níng　shàng diào　hún　sōng bǎi　fù gài
   府吏　为难　嫌　逼迫　叮咛　上吊　魂　松柏　覆盖

   mái zàng　yín　mèng jiāo　cí mǔ　féng yī　chūn huī
   埋葬　吟　孟郊　慈母　缝（衣）　春晖

3. gù dìng　yīn yùn　gé lǜ　yán gé　gōng zhěng　dòng tīng　dēng lóu　yì céng
   固定　音韵　格律　严格　工整　动听　登楼　一层

   kāi kuò　lú shān　pù bù　fēng huǒ　sāo
   开阔　庐山　瀑布　烽火　搔

4. mò　pēng　qīng tīng　shèng xián　jì mò　xī shí　yàn　jìng zhí　gū zhuó
   莫　烹　倾听　圣贤　寂寞　昔时　宴　径（直）　沽酌

   qiú　chóu
   裘　愁

5. fá xīn　liǎng bìn　yōu　jiàn　jià chē　niǎn　jī　xiē　piān piān　chì　qiān　qū
   伐薪　两鬓　忧　贱　驾车　辗　饥　歇　翩翩　叱　牵　驱

   shā　líng　jì　jià　zhí
   纱　绫　系　（价）值

6. 念奴娇 淘 豪杰 公瑾 姿 纶巾 强虏

7. 钗头凤 酥 （情）绪 山盟（海誓） 锦 托 泪痕 残笺

斜 阑 咽

8. 凭 潇潇 啸 激烈 耻 犹 踏 匈奴 阙

9. 钩 梧桐 锁 剪 一番 滋味 零 干戈 寥落 （浮）萍

10. 颂 山巅 澎湃 掀 狂澜 宛转 （弯）曲 摇篮 扮演

体魄 屏障 浩荡 臂膀 哺育 滋长 榜样 一枚

邮票 新娘 坟墓

共计149个生词

生詞表（繁）

1. shōu jí　piān　guǎng fàn　fǎn yìng　yǐng xiǎng　bǐ　ài　xíng shì　làng màn　jī chǔ
   收集　篇　廣泛　反映　影響　彼　艾　形式　浪漫　基礎

   lí sāo　shū qíng　fàng zhú　bēi fèn　yǎn tì　jīn bu zhù　qiú suǒ　zhuī qiú　lǐ xiǎng
   離騷　抒情　放逐　悲憤　掩涕　禁不住　求索　追求　理想

   zāo yù　guì zú　mìng yùn　shuāi luò　jì niàn　zòng zi
   遭遇　貴族　命運　衰落　紀念　粽子

2. xù shì　liú lán zhī　chún zhēn　bēi jù　pái huái　bàn lǚ　qín láo　lǎng sòng　jià
   敘事　劉蘭芝　純真　悲劇　徘徊　伴侶　勤勞　（朗）誦　嫁

   fǔ lì　wéi nán　xián　bī pò　dīng níng　shàng diào　hún　sōng bǎi　fù gài
   府吏　為難　嫌　逼迫　叮嚀　上吊　魂　松柏　覆蓋

   mái zàng　yín　mèng jiāo　cí mǔ　féng yī　chūn huī
   埋葬　吟　孟郊　慈母　縫（衣）　春暉

3. gù dìng　yīn yùn　gé lǜ　yán gé　gōng zhěng　dòng tīng　dēng lóu　yì céng
   固定　音韻　格律　嚴格　工整　動聽　登樓　一層

   kāi kuò　lú shān　pù bù　fēng huǒ　sāo
   開闊　廬山　瀑布　烽火　搔

4. mò　pēng　qīng tīng　shèng xián　jì mò　xī shí　yàn　jìng zhí　gū zhuó
   莫　烹　傾聽　聖賢　寂寞　昔時　宴　徑（直）　沽酌

   qiú　chóu
   裘　愁

5. fá xīn　liǎng bìn　yōu　jiàn　jià chē　niǎn　jī　xiē　piān piān　chì　qiān　qū
   伐薪　兩鬢　憂　賤　駕車　輾　饑　歇　翩翩　叱　牽　驅

   shā　líng　jì　jià　zhí
   紗　綾　繫　（價）值

91

中国诗歌欣赏

6. 念奴嬌 淘 豪傑 公瑾 姿 綸巾 強虜

7. 釵頭鳳 酥 (情)緒 山盟(海誓) 錦 託 淚痕 殘 箋

   斜 闌 嚥

8. 憑 瀟瀟 嘯 激烈 恥 猶 踏 匈奴 闕

9. 鈎 梧桐 鎖 剪 一番 滋味 零 干戈 寥落 (浮)萍

10. 頌 山巔 澎湃 掀 狂瀾 宛轉 (彎)曲 搖籃 扮演

    體魄 屏障 浩盪 臂膀 哺育 滋長 榜樣 一枚

    郵票 新娘 墳墓

共計149個生詞

第一课

一 写生词

篇												
广泛											
反映											
彼												
艾												
基础											
离骚											
抒情											
放逐											
悲愤											
掩												
涕												
禁不住										

求	索										
遭	遇										
衰	落										
粽	子										

二　组词

基_____　　抒_____　　遭_____　　逐_____

愤_____　　掩_____　　篇_____　　索_____

粽_____　　衰_____　　泛_____　　禁_____

三　选字组词

（构　沟）成　　　　　浪（慢　漫）

河（构　沟）　　　　　快（慢　漫）

四　抄写诗歌《采葛》一遍

_____

_____

_____

五 抄写诗句"路漫漫其修远兮,吾将上下而求索"两遍

_____

_____

六 根据课文选择正确答案

1. 《诗经》是中国第一部_____。

   A 历史书　　　　　B 诗歌总集　　　　C 小说

2. 《诗经》大约成书于_____。

   A 公元6世纪　　　B 公元600年　　　C 公元前6世纪

3. 《采葛》选自_____。

   A《诗经》　　　　　B《楚辞》

4. 屈原是_____楚国人。

   A 春秋时期　　　　B 战国时期

5. 屈原是中国第一位伟大的诗人。他创造了新的诗歌形式_____。

   A 楚辞　　　　　　B 诗经

6. 屈原的作品中最著名的是_____。

    A《诗经》　　　　B《离骚》

7. 中国诗歌的源头是由_____共同构成的。

    A《离骚》　　　　B《诗经》　　　　C《楚辞》与《诗经》

8. 端午节是为了纪念屈原,主要活动有_____。

    A 舞狮　　　　　　B 吃饺子　　　　　C 赛龙船、吃粽子

七 背诵并默写

1. 《采葛》。

2. 诗句"路漫漫其修远兮,吾将上下而求索"。

第三课

一 写生词

音	韵											
格	律											
登												
楼												
庐	山											
瀑	布											
烽	火											
搔												

二 组词

音_____   格_____   登_____   楼_____

三 抄写下列诗歌一遍

登鹳(guàn)雀楼

望庐山瀑布

春望

四 任选《登鹳雀楼》或《望庐山瀑布》中一首翻译成白话

五　选词填空

　　　　　　　　huàn　　　　fǔ
　　　　李白　　　王之涣　　　杜甫　　　白居易

　　　　五言律诗　　　七言绝句　　　五言绝句

1. 《登鹳雀楼》的作者是_____。

2. 《望庐山瀑布》的作者是_____。

3. 《春望》的作者是_____。

4. 《登鹳雀楼》是一首_____。

5. 《望庐山瀑布》是一首_____。

6. 《春望》是一首_____。

7. 唐代最著名的诗人有_____、_____和_____等。

六　词语解释

1. 依——

2. 欲——

3. 尽——

4. 穷——

5. 短——

6. 浑——

七 连线

五言绝句　　　　　全诗四句，每句七字

七言绝句　　　　　全诗八句，每句五字

五言律诗　　　　　全诗四句，每句五字

七言律诗　　　　　全诗八句，每句七字

八 背诵并默写《登鹳雀楼》和《望庐山瀑布》两首诗。（"鹳"字可以写拼音）

第五课

一 写生词

伐	薪										
两	鬓										
忧											
贱											
驾	车										
辗											
饥											
歇											
翩	翩										
叱											
牵											

驱											
纱											
绫											
系											
价	值										

二 组词

伐_____   系_____   忧_____   驾_____

鬓_____   牵_____   歇_____   饥_____

贱_____

三 选字组词

伐(薪 新)　　(饥 几)饿　　(代 伐)木

(薪 新)书　　(饥 几)个　　古(伐 代)

(纱 沙)布　　贵(贱 浅)　　价(植 值)

(纱 沙)土　　深(贱 浅)　　(植 值)物

四 抄写《卖炭翁》前八行

_____
_____
_____
_____
_____
_____
_____

五 反义词填空

饱　放心　贵

贱——（　　） 饥——（　　） 担忧——（　　）

六 选择填空

1.多吃有_____的食物有利于身体健康。

（营养　经营）

2.这个书店_____得很好,来买书的人越来越多。

（营养　经营）

3. 妹妹把新衣服弄脏了，真_____。　　（可惜　爱惜）

4. 小华十分_____她的书。　　　　　（可惜　爱惜）

5. 卖炭翁的作者是_____。（李白　杜甫(fǔ)　白居易）

七　根据课文判断对错

1. 卖炭翁卖炭的钱准备用来盖房子。　　　___对　___错

2. 卖炭翁穿的衣服很少。　　　　　　　　___对　___错

3. 为了炭能卖得贵一些，卖炭翁希望天气寒冷。　　　　　　　　　　　　　　　___对　___错

4. 卖炭翁进城一会儿就把炭卖完了。　　　___对　___错

5. 来了两个骑马的老百姓要买炭。　　　　___对　___错

6. 一车炭重量不到一千斤。　　　　　　　___对　___错

7. 半匹红纱、一丈绫与一车炭的价值一样。___对　___错

八 造句

    1. 担忧_____

    2. 价值_____

    3. 饥饿_____

九 背诵并默写《卖炭翁》前八句

第七课

一 写生词

钗												
酥												
情	绪											
山	盟											
锦												
托												
泪	痕											
残												
笺												
斜												
阑												
咽												

二 组词

钗_____ 盟_____ 绪_____ 痕_____

锦_____ 托_____ 斜_____ 咽_____

三 抄写陆游的《钗头凤》一遍（左边写上阕^{què}）

钗头凤（陆游）

_____ _____
_____ _____
_____ _____
_____ _____
_____ _____

四 抄写唐琬^{wǎn}的《钗头凤》一遍（左边写上阕^{què}）

钗头凤（唐琬）

_____ _____
_____ _____

五 根据课文选择正确答案

1. 陆游是_____人。

   A 汉朝　　　B 唐朝　　　C 南宋

2. 陆游的《钗头凤》是一首_____。

   A 诗　　　　B 词　　　　C 楚辞

六 词语解释

1. 一怀愁绪——

2. 泪痕残——

3. 离索——

4. 晓风——

七 背诵《钗头凤》（陆游）

八 默写《钗头凤》（陆游）第一段（生字可以写拼音）

第九课

一 写生词

钩											
梧桐											
锁											
剪											
一番											
滋味											
零											
干戈											
寥落											
浮萍											

二 组词

钩_____ 锁_____ 剪_____ 滋_____

戈_____ 番_____ 萍_____ 梧_____

三 抄写《相见欢》和《过零丁洋》

相见欢

过零丁洋

_____

_____

四 根据课文选择正确答案

1.《相见欢》(无言独上西楼)的作者是_____。

  A 李白   B 李煜(yù)

2.李煜是南唐的_____。

  A 皇帝   B 将军

3."人生自古谁无死,留取丹心照汗青"是_____的诗句。

  A 文天祥(xiáng)   B 岳飞

五 词语解释

1. 逢——

2. 身世——

3. 四周星——

4. 汗青——

六 把《相见欢》和《过零丁洋》中你喜欢的句子写下来
（每首选四句，左右分别写）

_____　　_____

_____　　_____

_____　　_____

_____　　_____

七 背诵《相见欢》和《过零丁洋》

八 默写《相见欢》后四句和《过零丁洋》最后两句

第一课听写

第三课听写

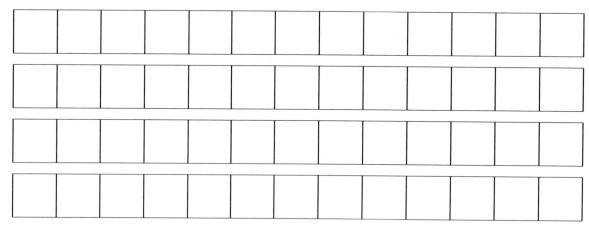

第五课听写

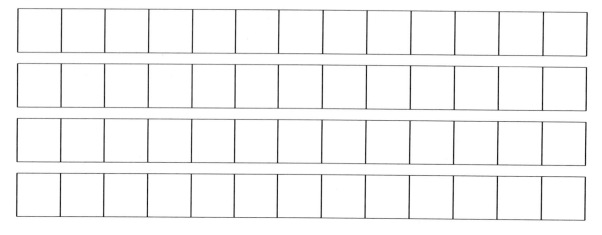

第七课听写

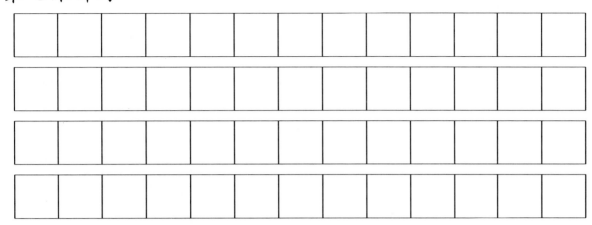

第九课听写

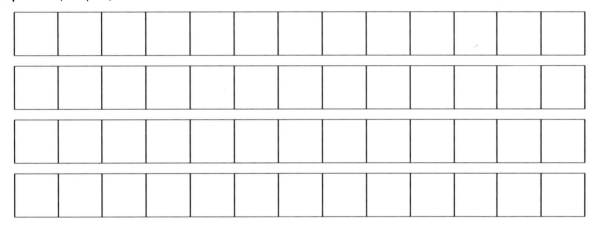

第二课

一　写生词

叙	事										
焦											
刘	兰	芝									
纯	真										
徘	徊										
伴	侣										
勤	劳										
朗	诵										
嫁											
府	吏										
嫌											
逼	迫										

叮	咛											
上	吊											
魂												
松	柏											
覆	盖											
埋	葬											
吟												
郊												
慈	母											
晖												

二 组词

徘_____ 诵_____ 勤_____ 迫_____

慈_____ 侣_____ 纯_____ 郊_____

葬_____ 覆_____ 柏_____ 叙_____

三 选字组词

（朗　郎）诵　　　　官（史　吏）　　　　（歉　嫌）弃

女（朗　郎）　　　　历（史　吏）　　　　道（歉　嫌）

四 抄写诗歌《游子吟》一遍，并翻译成白话

游子吟

_____　　　_____

_____　　　_____

_____　　　_____

译文：

_____

_____

_____

_____

_____

_____

五 将《孔雀东南飞》下列两段诗句翻译成白话

十七为君妇

心中常苦悲

鸡鸣入机织

夜夜不得息

三日断五匹

大人故嫌迟

六 根据课文选择正确答案

1. 乐府开始于_____。

  A 汉代   B 战国   C 春秋

2.《孔雀东南飞》是_____。

  A 汉乐府诗   B 楚辞   C 诗经

3.《游子吟》的作者是_____。

  A 屈原   B 孟郊

七 词语解释

1. 临行——

2. 晖——

3. 迟——

4. 心急如火——

八 背诵《游子吟》

第四课

一 写生词

莫												
烹												
倾	听											
圣	贤											
寂	寞											
昔	时											
宴												
径	直											
沽												
酌												
裘												
愁												

二 组词

宴_____ 圣_____ 倾_____ 烹_____

昔_____ 愁_____ 寂_____ 贤_____

三 抄写诗歌《将进酒》前八句

四 填空组词

      会   听   贤

宴_____   圣_____   倾_____

五 根据课文选择正确答案

1. 《将进酒》的作者是_____。

  A 杜甫   B 李白   C 白居易

2. "君不见高堂明镜悲白发,朝如青丝暮成雪"意思是_____。

  A 在镜子中看到自己头发白了

  B 感到时间过得飞快,人生短暂

3. "天生我材必有用,千金散尽还复来"意思是_____。

  A 自信有能力成就大事业,并不在乎金钱

  B 花钱大方

六　词语解释

　　1. 君——

　　2. 昔时——

　　3. 圣贤——

　　4. 烹——

　　5. 裘——

七　把诗歌《将进酒》中你喜欢的句子写下来

_____

_____

_____

_____

_____

_____

_____

八　背诵并默写《将进酒》前八句

第六课

一 写生词

奴												
淘												
豪	杰											
公	瑾											
姿												
纶	巾											
虏												

二 组词

壁_____ 淘_____ 豪_____ 杰_____

姿_____ 虏_____ 涛_____ 奴_____

三 选字组词

雄（次　姿）　　（毫　豪）杰　　回（家　嫁）

一（次　姿）　　（毫　豪）毛　　（家　嫁）女儿

四 抄写《念奴娇·赤壁怀古》一遍（左边写上阕(què)）

念奴娇·赤壁怀古

五 根据课文选择正确答案

1. 《念奴娇·赤壁怀古》的作者是_____。

   A 杜甫　　　　B 李白　　　　C 苏轼

2. 《念奴娇·赤壁怀古》是_____。

   A 唐诗　　　　B 宋词　　　　C 楚辞

3. 苏轼是_____的大文学家。

   A 战国时期　　B 宋朝　　　　C 唐朝

六 词语解释

1. 怀古——

2. 风流人物——

3. 强虏——

4. 豪杰——

七 把《念奴娇·赤壁怀古》中你喜欢的句子再写一遍

_____

_____

_____

八 背诵《念奴娇·赤壁怀古》

九 默写《念奴娇·赤壁怀古》中你喜欢的句子（不少于四句）

第八课

一 写生词

凭											
潇	潇										
啸											
激	烈										
耻											
犹											
踏											
匈	奴										
阙											

二 抄写《满江红·写怀》一遍（左边写上阕^{què}）

满江红·写怀

三 根据课文选择正确答案

    1.《满江红·写怀》的作者是_____。

       A 岳飞   B 苏轼   C 李白

2. 岳飞是_____人。

   A 汉朝　　　　B 唐朝　　　　C 宋朝

3. "莫等闲、白了少年头，空悲切"的意思是_____。

   A 年龄很小头发就白了，很悲伤

   B 不要叫时光轻易流走，结果一事无成而悲伤

4. 《满江红·写怀》表达了岳飞_____。

   A 希望报仇雪恨、收回国土的悲壮心情

   B 收复国土的快乐心情

四　词语解释

1. 怒发冲冠——

2. 潇潇——

3. 壮怀激烈——

4. 胡虏——

五　背诵《满江红·写怀》

六 默写《满江红·写怀》第一段

第十课

一 写生词

颂											
山巅											
澎湃											
掀											
狂澜											
宛转											
弯曲											
体魄											
屏障											
浩荡											
臂膀											
哺育											

榜	样										
一	枚										
邮	票										
坟	墓										

二 组词

颂_____   澎_____   掀_____   狂_____

扮_____   曲_____   榜_____   魄_____

屏_____   浩_____   臂_____   坟_____

票_____   邮_____   摇_____   坚_____

三 选字组词

(浩 告)荡　　(旁 榜)边　　(分 扮)演

(浩 告)诉　　(旁 榜)样　　(分 扮)开

(漂 票)亮　　(邮 油)寄　　(坟 蚊)墓

邮(漂 票)　　石(邮 油)　　(坟 蚊)子

中国诗歌欣赏

四 抄写《黄河颂》选段和《乡愁》全诗一遍（左起从上向下写）

啊！黄河！

你是中华民族的摇篮！

五千年的古国文化，

从你这儿发源；

多少英雄的故事，

在你身边扮演！

乡愁

五 根据课文选择正确答案

1.《黄河颂》的作者是_____。

　　A 光未然　　　　　B 余光中

2.《黄河颂》歌颂了_____。

　　A 黄河的壮观和古老

　　B 中华民族永不屈服的精神

3.《黄河大合唱》写于_____。

　　A 宋朝　　　　　　B 抗日战争时期

4.《乡愁》的作者是_____。

　　A 光未然　　　　　B 余光中

5.《乡愁》抒发了作者_____的感情。

　　A 思念母亲　　　　B 思念故乡和亲人

六 朗诵《黄河颂》、《乡愁》各三遍

第二课听写

第四课听写

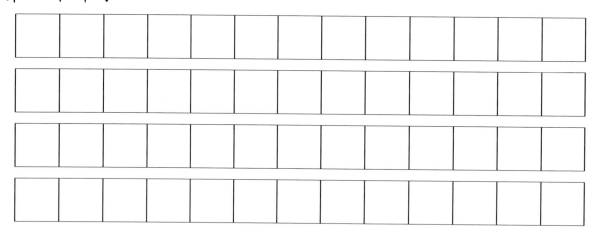

第六课听写

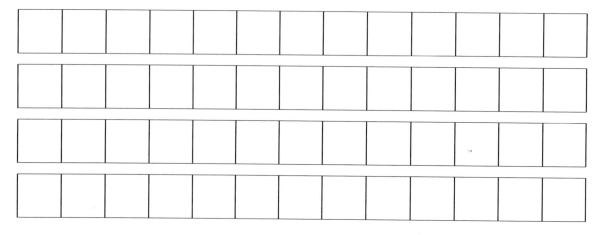

第八课听写

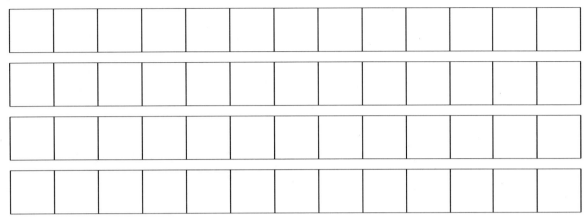

第十课听写

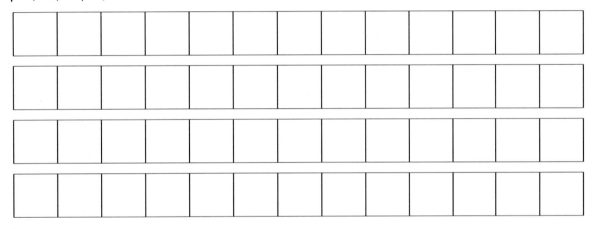